Can You Find It Outside?

Can You Find It Outside?

Jessica Schulte

THE METROPOLITAN MUSEUM OF ART

Harry N. Abrams, Inc., Publishers

Published in 2005 by The Metropolitan Museum of Art, New York, and Harry N. Abrams, Incorporated, New York
Copyright © 2005 by The Metropolitan Museum of Art

First Edition
Printed in China
14 13 12 11 10 09 08 07 06 05   5 4 3 2 1

Produced by the Department of Special Publications, The Metropolitan Museum of Art:
Robie Rogge, Publishing Manager; Jessica Schulte, Project Editor; Anna Raff, Designer; Gillian Moran, Production Associate.
Photography by The Metropolitan Museum of Art Photograph Studio.

Visit the Museum's Web site: www.metmuseum.org

Library of Congress Cataloging-in-Publication Data

Schulte, Jessica.
   Can you find it outside? / by Jessica Schulte.— 1st ed.
      p. cm.
   Includes bibliographical references and index.
   ISBN 0-8109-5795-7 (alk. paper)
   1. Painting—Themes, motives. 2. Painting—Appreciation. 3. Art—New York (State)—New York. 4.
Metropolitan Museum of Art (New York, N.Y.) I. Metropolitan Museum of Art (New York, N.Y.) II. Title.
   ND1143.S364 2005
   759—dc22

                                                                        2005000991

ISBN 1–58839–136–1 (MMA)
ISBN 0–8109–5795–7 (Abrams)

Harry N. Abrams, Inc.
100 Fifth Avenue
New York, NY 10011
www.abramsbooks.com

Abrams is a subsidiary of

LA MARTINIÈRE
GROUPE

INTRODUCTION

Here are thirteen paintings from the collections of The Metropolitan Museum of Art that tell stories, hold surprises, and beckon the youngest readers to look again and again at each work of art.

Every painting in this book shows a different outdoor scene that contains colorful details to pore over. Some of the scenes, like the one depicted in Vincent van Gogh's *First Steps, After Millet*, are of everyday places that children will know, from the marketplace and a snowy hill to the beach.

Others are fanciful. Edward Hicks's *Peaceable Kingdom* shows the lion lying down with the lamb. *Rip Van Winkle* illustrates that magical moment when Rip wakes up from his long slumber.

Each painting is accompanied by rhymes that guide readers, giving clues regarding the location of specific details. To keep the game going, there are even more objects to find listed at the bottom of the pages. But there's no reason for readers to stop there. They can keep searching to see what else might be "hidden" in the painting.

Youngsters will love being sent on a treasure hunt through art—the prize is in the looking!

—Jessica Schulte

If you look and if you stare,
There's a girl with long blond hair.

Can you find it? Can you see
A distant sailboat out at sea?

Look up there, but not too high!
What is flying in the sky?

Keep looking. Can you
also find two caps, white
stripes, and black buttons?

Can you find, in darkest night,
Houses lit with golden light?

Can you see? They're moving fast!
A horse and rider gallop past.

If you look above the people,
Can you find a tall white steeple?

Keep looking. Can you
also find chimneys, open
doors, and a person
leaning out a window?

You can find them if you choose.
Someone's wearing old brown shoes.

If you look, what do you see?
Daddy waits on bended knee.

Take a harder look around,
And find a shovel on the ground.

Keep looking. Can you also
find a fence, some flowers,
and a bonnet?

Can you find him and reveal
A little boy and his pinwheel?

If you look and if you wish,
You can find a tub of fish.

Squint your eyes. Now open wide!
Search out barrels by seaside.

Keep looking. Can you
also find striped shirts,
an umbrella, and carrots?

Do you see him stare at you?
A golden lion is in view.

If you search among the crowd,
You'll find a lamb, white as a cloud.

Can you find him? Yes, you can!
A great leopard joins the clan.

Keep looking. Can you
also find a hole in a tree,
a goat, and two bare feet?

ISAIAH 11 Chap 6 &c

Can you find it? Look about.
A fancy hat has fallen out.

Look here! Look there! Can you say
How many horses lead the way?

There's more to see! There's more to do!
Point to a lady wrapped in blue.

Keep looking. Can you
also find a river, blue
wheels, and some writing?

Can you find it? Do you see?
A chicken perches by a tree.

Not so far, now look nearby
And see a horse who's staying dry.

Now get ready and get set
To find a wagon getting wet.

Keep looking. Can you also find a man, a hanging wheel, and apples?

Can you find them? Can you try?
Yellow boats are gliding by.

If you watch the river race,
You'll see a mustache on a face.

If you're able, with some luck,
You just might find a swimming duck.

Keep looking. Can you also
find reflections in the water, a
red boat, and two bridges?

So much to see, so much to do,
Can you find the number two?

Hunt again. Look high and low.
Do you see a big green bow?

Search the crowd from side to side.
A baby's mouth is open wide.

Keep looking. Can you also
find two bowls, a red box,
and eyeglasses?

If you look the way you should,
You'll find a man who's chopping wood.

In the snow you'll find a thrill:
Sledders zipping down a hill.

Can you find him, brown and white,
A dog who runs with all his might?

Keep looking. Can you also find
a basket of vegetables, two people
going for a walk, and a fence?

Near the crowd—look carefully.
Find a man against a tree.

Look up front, look toward the sky.
Can you find a flag raised high?

Look at who has just appeared.
Do you see his long white beard?

Keep looking. Can you
also find two blue topcoats,
a barn, and a red dress?

Can you find it? You are bound
To spy a backpack on the ground.

Search the scene, don't use a map
To find a girl who takes a nap.

Take a look, now find and seek—
Where's the highest mountain peak?

Keep looking. Can you also
find a bag slung over a shoulder,
a pipe, and a walking stick stuck
in the ground?

The works of art reproduced in this book are from the collections of The Metropolitan Museum of Art, unless otherwise noted.

Eagle Head, Manchester, Massachusetts (High Tide)
Winslow Homer, American, 1836–1910
Oil on canvas, 26 x 38 in., 1870
Gift of Mrs. William F. Milton, 1923   23.77.2

The Midnight Ride of Paul Revere
Grant Wood, American, 1892–1942
Oil on Masonite, 30 x 40 in., 1931
Arthur Hoppock Hearn Fund, 1950   50.117

First Steps, After Millet
Vincent van Gogh, Dutch, 1853–1890
Oil on canvas, 28½ x 35⅞ in., 1890
Gift of George N. and Helen M.
Richard, 1964   64.165.2

Market Place
Andree Ruellan, American, b. 1905
Oil on canvas, 28 x 42¼ in., 1939
George A. Hearn Fund, 1940   40.83

Peaceable Kingdom
Edward Hicks, American,
1780–1849
Oil on canvas, 17⅞ x 23⅞ in.,
circa 1830–32
Gift of Edgar William and
Bernice Chrysler Garbisch,
1970 1970.283.1

Travel by Stagecoach Near Trenton, New Jersey
Pavel Petrovich Svinin, American, 1787/88–1839
Watercolor, gouache, and pen and ink on off-white
wove paper, 6⅞ x 9 13/16 in., circa 1811–13
Rogers Fund, 1942 42.95.11

Rainstorm—Cider Mill
at Redding, Connecticut
George Harvey, American,
circa 1800–1878
Watercolor and gouache
on white wove paper,
8⅜ x 13⅝ in., circa 1840
Maria DeWitt Jesup Fund
and Morris K. Jesup Funds,
1991 1991.206

The Champion Single Sculls
(Max Schmitt in a Single Scull)
Thomas Eakins, American, 1844–1916
Oil on canvas, 32¼ x 46¼ in., 1871
Purchase, The Alfred N. Punnett Endowment Fund and
George D. Pratt Gift, 1934 34.92

The Ameya
Robert Blum, American,
1857–1903
Oil on canvas, 25 1/16 x 31 1/16 in.,
by 1893
Gift of Estate of Alfred
Corning Clark, 1904 04.31

Red School House (Country Scene)
George Henry Durrie, American, 1820–1863
Oil on canvas, 26 x 36¼ in., 1850–60
Lent by Peter H. B. Frelinghuysen

Rip Van Winkle
Albertis del Orient Browere, American, 1814–1887
Oil on canvas, 21⅛ x 25 in., 1833
Gift of Mr. and Mrs. S. Richard Krown and Family, 2002   2002.444

The Mountain
Balthus, French, 1908–2001
Oil on canvas, 98 x 144 in., 1937
Purchase, Gifts of Mr. and Mrs. Nate B. Spingold and Nathan
Cummings, Rogers Fund and The Alfred N. Punnett Endowment
Fund, by exchange, and Harris Brisbane Dick Fund, 1982   1982.530

BACK JACKET
Cider Making
William Sidney Mount, American, 1807–1868
Oil on canvas, 27 x 34⅛ in., 1840–41
Purchase, Bequest of Charles Allen Munn, by exchange, 1966   66.126